Our World of Information

What's it about?
Information Around Us

Claire Throp

Heinemann
LIBRARY

www.heinemannlibrary.co.uk
Visit our website to find out more information about Heinemann Library books.

To order:

☎ Phone +44 (0) 1865 888066

🖹 Fax +44 (0) 1865 314091

💻 Visit www.heinemannlibrary.co.uk

Edited by Charlotte Guillain and Catherine Veitch
Designed by Richard Parker
Original illustrations © Capstone Global Library
Illustrated by Darren Lingard
Picture research by Ruth Blair
Originated by Heinemann Library
Printed in China by South China Printing Company Ltd.

ISBN 978 0 431163 15 4 (hardback)
14 13 12 11 10
10 9 8 7 6 5 4 3 2 1

British Library Cataloguing in Publication Data

Throp, Claire.
What's it about? : information around us. -- (Our world of information)
001-dc22
A full catalogue record for this book is available from the British Library.

Acknowledgements

We would like to thank the following for permission to reproduce photographs: Alamy pp. **9** (© Jupiterimages/BananaStock), **10** (© Image Farm Inc.), **20** (© Thierry Cariou); © Capstone Publishers pp. **17**, **19** & **18** (Karon Dubke); Corbis pp. **5** (Jim Craigmyle), **7** (Mihai Barbu/Reuters), **12** (Roy McMahon), **13** (Alan Schein Photography), **14** (David P. Hall), **24** (Michel Touraine/Pixland), **25** (Marc Serota/Reuters), **27** (Rainer Holz/Zefa), **29** (PlainPicture); Getty Images p. **15** (Gen Nishino); iStockphoto p. **21** (© Mark Goddard); Photoshot p. **11** (Imagebroker.net), **22** (Bader-Butowski).

Cover photograph of a woman using a mobile on a busy street reproduced with permission of Corbis (Yang Liu).

Every effort has been made to contact copyright holders of material reproduced in this book. Any omissions will be rectified in subsequent printings if notice is given to the publishers.

All the Internet addresses (URLs) given in this book were valid at the time of going to press. However, due to the dynamic nature of the Internet, some addresses may have changed, or sites may have changed or ceased to exist since publication. While the author and publisher regret any inconvenience this may cause readers, no responsibility for any such changes can be accepted by either the author or the publisher.

Contents

Any words appearing in the text in bold, **like this**, are explained in the glossary.

Information is everywhere

You are surrounded by information.
Information is what you know about things.
Information comes in many different forms.
It can be text, pictures, film, sounds, and
graphic organizers.

 There is information all around us. It
can be words we read, pictures we
see, or sounds we hear.

Information is everywhere. Information can be found on Internet pages, or in a list of phone numbers. Information can be heard through the radio or by the school bell ringing for the start of the day.

 Information can be found on mobile phones.

Why is information presented in different ways?

Information needs to be presented in different ways so that many people can understand it. Some information is easier to understand when it is written out. Other information is easier to understand when it is in a chart or graph.

Method	Speed (kilometres per hour)
Walking	5
Cycling	24
Driving car in town	40
Driving car on highway/ motorway	104

Graphic organizers, like this table, are good for showing certain types of information.

The siren on a fire engine makes a loud noise so that people can hear it even if they are in a car listening to music. **Visually impaired** people may not see signs or **symbols**. When they cross the road, visually impaired people may listen for a beeping noise made when the lights change to green.

 Emergency vehicles need a siren as well as flashing lights so you know they are coming before you see them.

How do different types of information affect us?

Information can affect you in many ways. When a word has been made bold in printed information, this tells you that the word is important.

Warning: Keep this product in a refrigerator.

 Food labels help you stay healthy by telling you when and how you should eat your food.

Some information can be enjoyed, such as when you listen to a story or watch a film.

Some information tells us to do things straightaway. For example, when you hear a fire alarm you need to get out of the building quickly.

Signs

Signs are a common source of information. The information can be shown through a sign's colour or shape. People who speak different languages can all understand what colours and shapes mean.

Warning signs are often shown in triangles.

10

 Many countries have the same signs for toilets.

Pictures on signs are usually very simple so people can easily understand them. A picture of a woman is usually used to show the women's toilets. A picture of a person in a wheelchair shows that there is access for disabled people.

Signs with words

 This sign tells people that the shop is closed.

Signs with words can give information such as the name of a school or the opening times of a library. Other signs can have pictures and words, such as a billboard. A billboard is a big sign used to **advertise** a **product** such as a type of food.

The size of the text on a sign depends on how far away people are likely to see it. For example, a sign that people need to see from a distance will have to use very large letters so they can read it.

 Billboards can be seen from quite a distance.

At home

Information can be found all around you, even at home. Your parents may have put a chart on the wall for household chores. This is so that everyone knows when it is their turn to clean out the pet cage or help with the dishes.

 Using a chart for household chores means that you will never forget to do your share.

Calendars are useful for everyone in the family.

A calendar shows the days, weeks, and months in a year. Calendars are useful because they help you keep track of what you are supposed to be doing each day. This means you can make sure you never miss swimming practice or football club.

Packaging

CAUTION: Use with adequate ventilation. In case of eye contact, flush immediately with water for at least 15 minutes.

CAUTION: Causes eye and skin irritation. Do not get in eyes, on skin, or on clothing.

⚠ DANGER

CONTENTS ARE FLAMMABLE: Keep spray away from heat, sparks, pilot lights, open flames, etc. Unplug electrical tools, motors, and other appliances before spraying or bringing the can near any source of electricity.

 Many **products** have warning labels that tell you how to use the product safely. Always ask an adult to handle these products.

Lots of information can be found on packaging. For example, if you want to find out what ingredients are in your favourite food, you can look at the packaging. Food labels give information about the food, including how to cook and store it.

Safety information might be shown on the box that a new toy comes in. It might be shown in bold letters, **like this**, so that it stands out as important.

ADVERTENCIA: PELIGRO DE ASFIXIA – PIEZAS PEQUEÑAS.
No para niños menores de 3 años.

WARNHINWEIS: ERSTICKUNGSGEFAHR – KLEINTEILE.
Nicht geeignet für Kinder unter 3 Jahren.

AVVERTENZA: PERICOLO DI SOFFOCAMENTO – CONTIENE PICCOLE PARTI. Non adatto per bambini al di sotto di 3 anni.

AVISO: PERIGO DE SUFOCAÇÃO – PEÇAS PEQUENAS.
Não se destina a crianças com menos de 3 anos de idade.

WAARSCHUWING: VERSTIKKINGSGEVAAR – KLEINE ONDERDELEN.
Niet geschikt voor kinderen onder 3.

47 pcs
pzs/pzas
3+

0-3

CONFORMS TO B.S. 5665/EN71

 The information on a toy box might tell you what age group the toy is meant for.

Books and newspapers

There is a lot of information in books and newspapers. If you look at a newspaper, there are many different sizes of text. The name of the newspaper is often the biggest, followed by the heading of the main story. The text used in the story itself is quite small.

Large text is designed to catch your eye and make you want to buy the newspaper and read the story.

Information can also be found in pictures. For example, photos can tell you what things look like. Sometimes you can find clues in pictures to help you work out what the text is about.

Food can make all kinds of tasty patterns. What patterns did you eat today?

 This book is probably about fruit and vegetables.

Electronic information

There are many different types of electronic information. The Internet is a connection between millions of computers, meaning lots of information can be shared. **Online encyclopedias** and dictionaries allow you to search for information on a wide range of subjects.

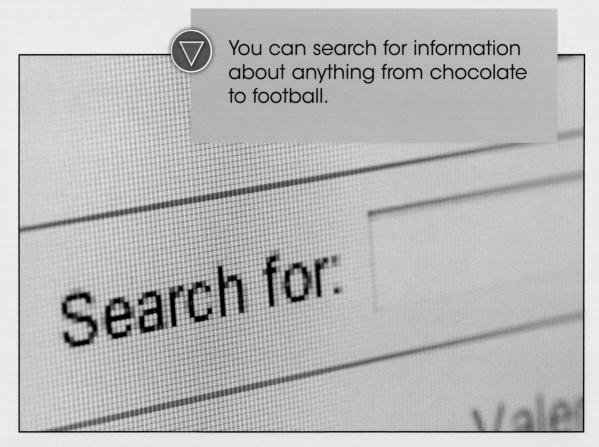

You can search for information about anything from chocolate to football.

Ask if you need help finding information.

You can also use **multi-media discs** to find information. Some other types of electronic or online information are text messages, blogs, **wikis**, social websites, and video or music websites. New types of electronic and online information appear each year.

Television and video

Television programmes and video can give information about many subjects that you are interested in. Television and video can also be found on the Internet. You can either watch live **streaming** of the videos or **download** videos to watch later.

Watching television can be fun, and it may also be a good place to learn new things.

Some television stations, such as the BBC, do not show adverts.

In between television shows there are sometimes a number of very short programmes called **adverts**. Adverts try to sell things to the people watching. Adverts give a different type of information to that found on the television programmes.

23

Sounds

Sounds can tell you information. An alarm clock rings so that you know it is time to get up in the morning. The theme tune of your favourite television programme lets you know that it is about to begin.

 Hearing the school bell lets you know that it is playtime.

You can often hear emergency vehicles before you can see them.

Sounds can also be warnings. For example, a siren warns drivers to get out of the way of a fire engine or an ambulance.

Information in our lives

Information is everywhere and is usually helpful to us. However, there is so much information in our world that it can sometimes feel hard to know where to look or what to do.

 It is important to learn which information is worth paying attention to and which is not.

Information is presented in different ways so that you can understand it. Information can help you make decisions and understand your world. Information can help you learn new things.

 Finding out new information can be fun.

Activities

Different information

Try spending a day looking out for different types of information. Before you go out, draw a simple table like the one below in a notebook. Take your notebook and pen with you and write down how many times you come across each type of information.

Text	Pictures	Text and pictures	Film	Sound

Get together with a friend
and try reading pictures.

Reading pictures

Look through a picture book with a friend and choose a picture. Each of you should try to write down three pieces of information from the picture. When you have finished, compare what you have written. Did you find the same information?

Glossary

advert made by companies to get people to buy the DVDs, toys, or other things they make. Information in adverts is usually one-sided.

advertise to tell people about something, often a product to be sold

download moving information from the Internet to a personal computer or other electronic equipment. For example, you can download a music track from a website to your computer. Before you download anything, ask an adult. Not all downloads are allowed or safe.

encyclopedia book with information about many subjects, or on a particular subject

graphic organizer way of showing information in a chart, table, or graph

multi-media disc disc that gives information in different forms such as sound, text, and video

online connected to the Internet

product something made by people, usually for selling. Toys or food are examples of products.

streaming when you can view information on the Internet straightaway without having to download it

symbol word or picture that stands for something else. For example, a triangle made up of three arrows is the sign for recycling.

visually impaired people who are unable to see very well or at all

wiki a website that allows many people to add or change information

Find out more

Books

My First Email Guide, Chris Oxlade (Heinemann Library, 2007)

My First Internet Guide, Chris Oxlade (Heinemann Library, 2007)

Websites

Yahoo! Kids – Homework Help
http://kids.yahoo.com/learn
This web page includes links to an encyclopedia, dictionary, maps, and lots of other useful websites.

CBBC Newsround
www.bbc.co.uk/cbbc/help/safesurfing
This BBC website gives you advice on staying safe while you are on the Internet.

Index